BULL HARRIS
and the Purple Ooze

Julie Mitchell   *Illustrated by* Rae Dale

sundance

A Haights Cross Communications Company

For information regarding permission, write to:
Sundance Publishing
234 Taylor Street
Littleton, MA   01460

Published by
Sundance Publishing
234 Taylor Street
Littleton, MA   01460

Copyright © text Julie Mitchell
Copyright © illustrations Rae Dale
Project commissioned and managed by
Lorraine Bambrough-Kelly, The Writer's Style
Cover and text design by Marta White

First published 1996 by
Addison Wesley Longman Australia Pty Limited
95 Coventry Street
South Melbourne 3205 Australia
Exclusive United States Distribution: Sundance Publishing

ISBN 0-7608-4955-2

PRINTED IN CANADA

Contents

Chapter 1

Bradley Finds a Brain

"Hand it over, Dunn!

"What?" I asked, pretending not to know what Bull Harris meant.

"You know what. That little speech of yours."

Bull grabbed a fistful of my T-shirt and yanked
my face up next to his. He was the biggest kid in
seventh grade—and the meanest. But I'd worked
hard on my speech for the school competition
and I wasn't going to give it up to anyone.

"You're not getting it," I said, amazed at how brave I sounded.

He laughed — and I had a close-up view of the huge gap between his front teeth. Bull was very proud of that gap. He was the only kid who could walk around the school with a quarter stuck between his two front teeth. Big deal.

He shoved me hard against the rail of the footbridge. "Brent! Jarrod! Get over here!" he ordered.

Two other kids from our class strode out
of the bushes and onto the bridge.

"Brought your army, huh, Bull?" I taunted.

He ignored me and ordered Brent and Jarrod to hold me while he searched my backpack.

"I know it's in here, Dunn," he said. "But I've got other things to do, so I'll just throw the whole lot overboard."

"Nooooo!" I yelled. But it was too late. My backpack flew through the air and nosedived into the creek.

"I guess that takes care of *your* speech," Bull gloated. "First prize is mine. I can taste that hamburger already."

The three of them walked back over the bridge, laughing.

"You won't win, Harris!" I yelled after him. "Nicole or Kylie could still beat you!"

He stopped and turned around. "Oh yeah. I suppose they could *if* they still had their speeches. But my good buddies here have already taken care of that."

So that was it. Bull Harris had won again.
I didn't care about not winning the free lunch for
the best speech. What made me sick was
knowing I wouldn't rat on Bull.

It had been tried once, but the kid who ratted had his mind changed by Bull's fists. The next day the kid told the teacher he'd made the whole thing up. The school was full of kids who kept their mouths shut.

I watched my backpack float for a while in the
middle of the creek, then it sank like a leaky boat.

Even if I could have rescued it, I would never have been able to get rid of the sewer smell.

Sorrow Creek had been polluted for years.

I walked off the bridge and sat on the bank.
I closed my eyes and tried to remember my
speech.

"Trees . . ." I said out loud, hoping the rest would follow. But all that came was a jumble of words like trunk, leaves, and shade. I would have to write a new speech and there wasn't time to make it good enough to beat Bull's. His dad had written his speech. But no one was going to tell the teacher, of course.

I opened my eyes again, and that's when I noticed it, an odd lump about the size of a hen's egg lying among the reeds. It was covered with black muck, so I picked up a stick and scraped it clean. Underneath the gunk was something pink, with purple, squiggly lines on it. It looked like it could be a model of a brain.

Now I have to tell you, I love collecting what my mother calls *ghastly things*.

In my bedroom I have a table covered with them — toy spiders, bats, vampires, werewolves, and monsters of all sorts. They're all arranged among some gravestones I made, and a big plastic eyeball sits in the middle. The brain would look great on the table. I wrapped it in my handkerchief and took it home.

When Mom finished telling me how long it would take to save up my pocket money to pay for a new backpack, I went into the bathroom and washed the brain.

It seemed to be made of rubber, yet it was quite
hard. Maybe Sorrow Creek had done something
to it. I used a toothbrush (not mine, of course)
to scrub between its bumps, then rubbed some
perfume all over it to get rid of the smell.

I found the perfect spot for it on my monster table — right in front, between Dracula and The Mummy.

I went to work on my speech. I'd returned all the books about trees to the library, so I had to write whatever came into my head.

After half-an-hour, I hadn't written much, just:

Trees have trunks and branches.

Some trees lose their leaves in winter.

Trees give shade to animals.

I could already hear Mr. Jensen saying, "Bradley, I'm afraid you don't have enough detail."

Time for a break. I walked over to my monster table and picked up the brain. It smelled good now and I liked the feel of it in my hand.

Closing my eyes, I tried again to remember my speech. In my mind there were pictures of trees, but that was all. I screwed my eyes shut tightly and squeezed my hands into fists, trying to force the memory to come.

Chapter 2

The Big Squeeze

Something strange happened; a tingling feeling traveled all over me, my eyes flicked open and I heard myself saying *exactly* what was in my speech.

My mouth was working on its own. And when I came to the end of my speech, I began to tell everything I ever knew, or thought, or felt about trees. I tried to stop myself, but I couldn't. I was like a faucet that wouldn't turn off.

My mouth closed and there was silence.
The brain lay on the floor. It had turned a
deep red and now was fading back to pink
as I watched.

Something amazing had happened when I squeezed it, and if I was right, that something was going to give me a chance to beat Bull Harris in the competition. I had to test my idea.

Dad was in the living room, watching *Sale of the Century*. I put the brain in his hand, curled his fingers around it, and squeezed hard.

"Brad, what on earth are you . . . ?" he began.

Then an odd look came over his face.
"*Sale of the Century* is a game where three
contestants try to answer questions in the fastest
time," he blurted out. "If you win, you can take
a fantastic prize home at the end of the show or
come back the next night and play again. I've
always wanted to go on *Sale of the Century* but
my wife told me I wasn't smart enough — *she*
should talk — so I've never. . ."

I stopped making his hand squeeze the brain.

"Goodness!" he said. "I can't think why I'd say such a thing! Your mother's a wonderful woman." Then he noticed he was holding a brain in his hand. He screwed up his face. "*That*, Bradley, is disgusting," he said, and dropped it in my lap.

I didn't care. I knew how it worked now. All you had to do to remember something was think about it and then squeeze the brain. You had to be careful to stop squeezing at the right moment, though, or you might say more than you wanted.

Bull Harris was in for a surprise.

At lunchtime the next day, I met with Kylie Atkins and Nicole Cheng, the other competitors.

"Mr. Jensen should never have made us bring our speeches to school yesterday," Kylie said. "Then Bull's buddies couldn't have taken them on the way home."

"They would have gotten you on the way to school today," I said.

A smile crept over my face. "Anyway, it doesn't matter now."

"What!" Nicole said. "I could've gotten eight or nine out of ten for mine, but now I'll be lucky to get three."

I took the brain out of my pocket and told them how it worked. Kylie laughed, but Nicole wanted to try it.

"Okay," I said. "If either of you wants to use it, just walk past me on the way up to the front and I'll hand it to you. But don't let Bull see it."

The bell rang and we went inside. I saw Bull pinch Dale Groves until he cried, and I wished again that I had the courage to rat.

Nicole was the first to give her speech.
She walked past me, and I handed her the brain.
"Good luck," I whispered.

"Mr. Jensen, girls and boys, my speech is about insects," she began.

Then I saw her clench her fist. She got an eight.

I heard Bull whisper angrily to Brent, "I thought you tore up her speech!"

"I did!" he hissed.

Nicole carefully passed the brain back to me as she returned to her seat. Then Kylie decided to try it and took it from me before she began her speech.

I looked at Bull. He wasn't happy, and by the time Kylie had finished her speech and been given a perfect ten, he was glaring at me.

Kylie needed to be extra careful not to let him see the brain when she handed it back to me.

And then the worst thing possible happened.

The brain was almost in my hand when Kylie noticed Bull's angry stare. It made her so nervous she dropped it, and it rolled across the floor.

"Cheat!" Bull Harris cried, and pounced on it straight away. "There must be a tape recorder hidden inside here!"

"Give it back!" I yelled, making a grab for it. "It's mine."

"Sit down, both of you!" Mr. Jensen ordered.

Bull wasn't listening. I knew he was already planning how to get me.

And while he thought about that, he held the brain above his head where I couldn't reach it. He was squeezing it so hard his knuckles were white.

Chapter 3

The Purple Ooze

The speech Bull gave that day was not the one he had planned to give. It had no title, but it might have been called *Getting People*. He sounded like a snarling animal as he described how he was going to make a punching bag out of me on the way home.

He told about all the other kids he had ever hurt or frightened. David Mace, who he'd beaten up for winning the bike raffle.

Karly Bolton, whose arm he had bitten for not letting him use her new colored pencils.

Smaller kids he had shoved off the slide because he wanted a turn.

And Brent and Jarrod, whose fingers he had bent backwards when they didn't do as he said.

The list went on and on.

All the while, Bull stood frozen with his arm in the air, his mouth the only moving part.
In his raised hand, the brain was changing shape and color. It began to ooze between his fingers.

As Bull went on, raving about the horrible things he'd done, purple sludge ran down his arm and over his shoulder.

It was as though the brain was drawing all the poison from inside Bull to the outside, then burying him in it.

When he was completely covered in purple ooze, he began to shrink.

There is a new monster on my table.

It stands right in the front, between Dracula and The Mummy, where the brain used to be. It's about fifteen inches tall. It's purple. And it has a gap between its teeth just big enough to hold a nickel.

About the Author
Julie Mitchell

Julie Mitchell was born in the Victorian country town of Korumburra where she grew up on a dairy farm. Julie moved to Frankston to become a primary school teacher and spent many years teaching students in schools on the Mornington Peninsula. Julie's favorite activity is to escape into a good book, especially fantasy or science fiction. Julie strongly believes that your imagination needs exercise. "It has to be let off the leash and taken for a run every now and then," she said.

About the Illustrator
Rae Dale

Rae Dale was born in Melbourne and now lives in the northeast hill country with her family. After obtaining her Diploma of Art from Swinburne Institute of Technology, she taught art for a few years in various schools. Since then, painting and illustrating are her major interests, as well as reading, gardening, washing dishes, and collecting proverbs.